Ducks on the Run!

Story by Annette Smith   Illustrations by Jenny Mountstephen

2

Grace and Amy were going fishing
with Mom and Dad.

On the way,
they drove through a forest.

"Look out!" said Mom.
"There are some birds
running along the road
ahead of us."

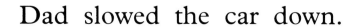

Dad slowed the car down.

"Oh!" said Grace.
"It's a mother duck
with her little ducklings."

"Why are they on the road?"
asked Amy.

"I think the mother duck
must be taking her family
to the lake," said Mom.

5

"We have to help them," said Grace,
"or they could get run over."

Dad stopped the car
at the side of the road,
and they all got out.

"I know what we can do," said Amy.
"We can catch them
in your fishing net, Dad.
Then we can take them
down to the lake."

Dad got the net from the car. He told the twins to stay on the side of the road where it was safe.

Mom watched for cars coming around the corner.

Dad crept slowly up behind the ducks.

He held out the net,
but the mother duck
ran faster than ever.

Dad swung the net down
over the mother duck
and he got her.
But the little ducklings
ran into the long grass
at the side of the road.

"Watch those ducklings!" shouted Dad.
"Don't let them get into the bushes,
or we will never find them."

Mom got an empty box
from the back of the car,
and Dad put the mother duck into it.

Grace and Amy
stayed by the ducklings.
They kept them in the long grass.

Then Dad crept along
the side of the road behind the ducklings.

He held the net up!

The little ducklings ran out
of the long grass.

And Dad trapped most of them
in the net.

"Oh, no!" said Grace.
"Dad, you missed one of them.
It has run into the bushes!"

"I'll watch where it goes," said Amy. "You help Dad with the others."

Grace kept the ducklings under the net, and then Dad put them into the box with their mother.

"Quick!" said Amy.

This time, Dad got the last little duckling in the net.

Then Mom and Dad and the twins
crossed the road.
Dad carried the box,
and they all went down the path
to the lake.

"There you are, Mother Duck,"
said Amy.
"You and your ducklings belong **here**,
not on the road."